Cornerstones of Freedom

The Liberty Bell

Gail Sakurai

CHILDREN'S PRESS®
A Division of Grolier Publishing
New York • London • Hong Kong • Sydney
Danbury, Connecticut

Library of Congress Cataloging-in-Publications Data

Sakurai, Gail.
   The Liberty Bell / by Gail Sakurai.
      p. cm.—(Cornerstones of freedom)
   Includes index.
      ISBN 0-516-06634-X
      1. Liberty Bell—Juvenile literature. I. Title. II. Series.
   F158.8.I3S27 1996
   974.8'11—dc20
                                                               95-17740
                                                                    CIP
                                                                     AC

Copyright ©1996 by Children's Press®, Inc.
All rights reserved. Published simultaneously in Canada.
Printed in the United States of America.
1 2 3 4 5 6 7 8 9 10 R 05 04 03 02 01 00 99 98 97 96

People crowd around the Liberty Bell. Everyone wants to see it and touch it.

An African-American man runs his finger along the crack in the bell. His ancestors were brought from Africa in chains. When their ships arrived in America, the Africans were sold as slaves. For him, the bell represents freedom from slavery.

An exchange student from Ukraine says, "I touched it. I touched the bell." She spent most of her life under communist rule. Now, she and her country are both free.

A thin, gray-haired woman pushes up her sleeve, revealing a mark on her arm. It identifies her as a survivor of the Nazi concentration camp, Auschwitz. "You see why the bell means so much to me," the woman says. For her, and for people all over the world, the Liberty Bell symbolizes freedom.

Civil rights figure Rosa Parks and Philadelphia Mayor Wilson Goode at the Liberty Bell in 1988.

When the Pennsylvania Assembly ordered a bell in 1751, they had no idea that it would become a national monument and a treasured symbol of liberty. The Assembly members were concerned only with practical matters. They needed a new bell for their State House in Philadelphia.

In the 1700s, bells were an important means of communication. Bells rang to call meetings, announce news, and signal danger, such as fire or enemy attack. Bells tolled to celebrate special occasions and to mourn the deaths of leading citizens.

There were no bell makers in or near Philadelphia in 1751. So, the Pennsylvania Assembly decided to order its bell from England. Isaac Norris, Speaker of the Assembly, sent a letter to London, dated November 1. He wrote that the Assembly wanted "a good Bell of about two thousand pounds weight." Norris instructed the bell makers to place an inscription on the bell. He chose a Bible verse—Leviticus, Chapter XXV, Verse 10: "Proclaim liberty throughout all the land unto all the inhabitants thereof."

By the next summer, the Assembly was growing impatient to receive its bell. Finally, it arrived by ship at the end of August.

The Liberty Bell's top line of engraved text is a quotation from the Bible.

On September 1, 1752, Norris wrote, "The bell is come ashore and in good order and we hope it will prove a good one."

The bell's arrival caused much excitement. Everyone was eager to hear it ring. A crowd gathered in the State House yard. They watched as workers unloaded the bell and hung it on a temporary frame. The spectators held their breaths as the clapper swung. A dreadful clanking noise filled the yard. The bell had cracked on the very first stroke!

The Assembly debated what should be done about the cracked bell. Isaac Norris reported, "We concluded to send it back by Captain Budden, but he could not take it on board." Captain Budden's ship, the *Myrtilla,* was already fully loaded.

It might be weeks, or even months, before another ship sailed for England. The Assembly did not want to wait that long for the bell. Fortunately, "two Ingenious Work-Men," John Pass and John Stow, agreed to recast the bell in Philadelphia.

Very little is known about Pass and Stow. John Pass was "a native of the isle of Malta," according to Isaac Norris. John Stow was a Philadelphia brass maker. He had a foundry on Second Street, where he sold "all sorts of brasses…at the most reasonable rates." Historians have not been able to learn if either man had any previous training or experience in bell casting.

Pass and Stow thought the bell had cracked because the metal was too brittle. They broke the bell into small pieces, melted it down, and added copper to the mixture to strengthen it. Then they poured the liquid metal into a mold and allowed it to harden.

By the end of March 1753, the new Pass and Stow bell was hanging in the State House belfry. The Assembly held a party for the first official bell ringing. The guests feasted on beef, ham, potatoes, cheese, bread, and punch made with three hundred limes.

Although the party was a great success, the bell ringing was not. The bell's tone was harsh and unmusical. The bell makers had added too much copper. People laughed and made jokes about the bell's sound.

Pass and Stow were "so tiezed with the witticisms of the town" that they took the bell down and recast it once more. This time they added tin to improve the tone. They worked night and day to finish the bell in record time. By early June, it hung in the steeple, ready to proclaim liberty throughout the land.

However, not everyone was completely satisfied with this bell's tone. Isaac Norris said, "Tho' some are of the opinion it will do, I Own I do not like it."

The Assembly considered replacing it with a new bell that Isaac Norris ordered from England. But

Pass and Stow produced a bell with an unpleasant ring, so they recast it (left). Pass and Stow's names are engraved on the Liberty Bell (below).

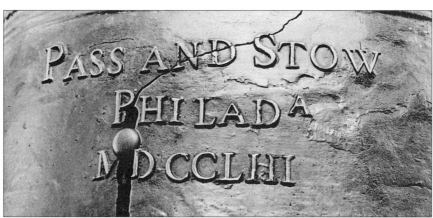

when the English bell arrived, it didn't sound any better than the Pass and Stow bell. The Assembly decided to place the new English bell in the clock tower, where it would chime the hours. The bell cast by Pass and Stow remained in the steeple, where it served as the official State House Bell.

The State House Bell immediately went to work. It announced meetings of the Pennsylvania Assembly and sessions of the Courts of Justice. It called citizens to the State House yard to hear news or discuss issues of the day. The bell rang so often that people began to complain about the noise.

In 1772, the Assembly received a petition from "divers inhabitants of the City of Philadelphia, living near the State House." The petition claimed that the people were "much incommoded and distressed by the too frequent Ringing by the great Bell in the Steeple of the State House, the inconvenience of which has often been felt severely when some of the Petitioners' families have been affected with sickness, at which times, from its uncommon size and unusual sound, it is extremely dangerous and may prove fatal."

The petitioners asked the Assembly to ring the bell less frequently. The Assembly ignored the petition and continued to ring the bell as often as before.

As the years passed, citizens of Pennsylvania and the other English colonies in America became increasingly upset with English rule. They greatly resented the series of restrictions and taxes the English king imposed on them. For instance, the colonists were forbidden to manufacture steel, iron, wool, and hats. They were not allowed to transport goods from one colony to another, or to trade with any country other than England. The Americans considered this treatment very unfair.

In addition, England placed taxes on various goods brought into the colonies, including molasses, glass, lead, paint, paper, and tea. Each time a new tax was imposed, the Americans protested angrily. They called it "taxation without representation." They claimed that the English government had no right to tax the colonies because the colonies had no representatives in the English government. The Americans refused to pay the taxes. The English king sent soldiers to force the colonists to obey.

The Boston Massacre of 1770 was one of many violent conflicts that led to the Revolutionary War.

By 1775, fighting had broken out between the colonists and the king's soldiers. Some people believed that the only solution to the conflict was to break free from England. The time for proclaiming liberty was drawing nearer.

In 1776, the Second Continental Congress was meeting in Philadelphia. Delegates came from all the thirteen English colonies in America. Among the delegates were John Adams, Samuel Adams, Benjamin Franklin, John Hancock, Thomas Jefferson, and many other important leaders of the time. They gathered at the State House to discuss the issue of independence. High above their heads, the old State House Bell waited in its belfry.

On July 2, Congress passed a resolution stating, "These United Colonies are, and of right ought to be, free and independent States."

On July 4, Congress approved the Declaration of Independence, a document written by Thomas Jefferson, the young delegate from Virginia. The Declaration listed the reasons for independence. It proclaimed that all people were entitled to "life, liberty, and the pursuit of happiness."

The signing of the Declaration of Independence on July 4, 1776

The Declaration of Independence is read to a crowd outside the Philadelphia State House (right). Afterward, the Liberty Bell was rung, declaring liberty for all (below).

On July 8, thousands of people crowded into the State House yard. At noon, Colonel John Nixon read the Declaration of Independence to the public for the first time. When he finished, the crowd cheered loudly.

Then the bell rang out joyfully, proclaiming liberty throughout the land, "to all the inhabitants thereof."

But liberty did not come easily. England was not willing to give up the colonies. The new United States was forced to fight for its independence. By the following summer, the war against England was not going well. Philadelphia was in constant danger of being captured. Even so, the bell pealed on the Fourth of July, 1777, to celebrate the first anniversary of independence.

As fall approached, the threat of English invasion grew. Congress feared that the city's bells would fall into enemy hands. The English army would almost certainly melt the bells to make ammunition. The bells had to be taken down, spirited out of the city, and hidden away. By the time the English marched into Philadelphia on September 26, 1777, all the bells were gone.

Colonel Benjamin Flower was in charge of getting the bells to safety. He hid them in farm wagons under a cover of straw and old sacks. The State House Bell rode in the wagon belonging to farmer John Jacob Mickley.

In 1777, the Liberty Bell was hidden outside Philadelphia from advancing British troops.

Outside Philadelphia, the farm wagons joined a convoy of seven hundred American army wagons. When the wagon train arrived in the small town of Bethlehem, Pennsylvania, Mickley's wagon broke down. The State House Bell was transferred to Frederick Leaser's farm wagon. Leaser drove the bell the rest of the way to Northampton (present-day Allentown, Pennsylvania). In Northampton, the bell was hidden beneath the floor of the Zion Reformed Church. The Church's pastor, the Reverend Abraham Blumer, helped to lower the bell into its hiding place.

The bell remained in hiding until the English left Philadelphia on June 18, 1778. Then, it returned to the State House steeple. By 1781, the wooden steeple had rotted and needed to be torn down. Workers lowered the bell to the brick part of the tower, where it remained for the next seventy years. But the bell was heard on October 24, 1781, when it pealed joyfully to announce the surrender of the English army at Yorktown, Virginia. The Americans had won the Revolutionary War. When the formal peace treaty was finally signed in 1783, the bell rang out again.

Four years later, delegates to the Constitutional Convention met at the State House in Philadelphia. After months of debate and compromise, they wrote a new plan of government for the United States and called it the Constitution. One of its goals was to "secure the Blessings of Liberty to

The signing of the U.S. Constitution

These fireworks (below) are a spectacular background for the replica of the Liberty Bell that sits atop Veteran's Stadium in Philadelphia.

ourselves and our Posterity." The delegates adopted the Constitution on September 17, 1787.

Nine of the thirteen states had to approve the Constitution for it to become law. Delaware was the first, on December 7, 1787, followed by Pennsylvania, New Jersey, Georgia, Connecticut, Massachusetts, Maryland, and South Carolina. The ninth state, New Hampshire, approved the Constitution on June 21, 1788, and Virginia joined in on June 26. A week later, Philadelphia joyfully celebrated on the Fourth of July, with parades, fireworks, and speeches. Once more the bell rang out, proclaiming liberty throughout the land.

For many years, the Liberty Bell continued its duties for both Pennsylvania and the United States. Then in 1799, Pennsylvania transferred its state capital to Lancaster. A year later, the United States government moved to the new capital city of Washington, D.C. The State House was empty. The bell's daily duties were over, but it still rang for special occasions. It pealed to welcome important visitors. It tolled for the deaths of famous people. And it repeated its message of liberty every year on July Fourth.

In the following decades, the State House Bell narrowly escaped destruction twice. The first near-disaster occurred in 1816. That year, the Pennsylvania legislature needed funds to build a new state capitol in Harrisburg. To raise the money, the legislators wanted to tear down the old State House and sell the land it stood on. The bell would have been either sold or discarded. Luckily, the city of Philadelphia came to the rescue. The city bought the State House, its land, and its contents, including the bell, for $70,000.

In 1828, the bell was threatened once more. The city of Philadelphia had decided to preserve the State House as a historical monument. City officials planned to repair the State House, rebuild the steeple, and install a clock in the new steeple. They hired John Wilbank, a bell maker, to cast a new bell for the clock. They offered him the old bell as scrap metal.

Fortunately, Wilbank thought it was too much trouble to carry away the heavy old bell. He left it hanging in its brick tower. The bell was safe again—temporarily.

Seven years later, disaster struck. On July 8, 1835, while tolling for the death of Chief Justice John Marshall, the Liberty Bell cracked.

John Marshall was the first chief justice of the Supreme Court. Upon his death in 1835, the Liberty Bell was rung. Unfortunately, the bell cracked on that occasion.

Christ Church (left) and St. Peter's Cathedral (right) still stand in historic Philadelphia. An 1846 dispute between the two churches led to a compromise that called for the Liberty Bell to be rung on George Washington's birthday.

For many years, the broken bell hung in its tower, silent and forgotten. Then, in 1846, a dispute arose between two churches. Both Christ Church and St. Peter's Church claimed the honor of ringing their bells to celebrate George Washington's birthday. Christ Church wanted the sole honor—and the entire thirty dollar fee—all to itself. St. Peter's was willing to share both the honor and the payment. Half of Philadelphia's city council supported Christ Church, while the other half was firmly on St. Peter's side. Finally, a newspaper writer suggested ringing the old State House Bell instead, and the city leaders agreed.

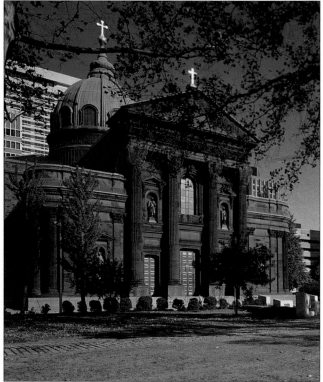

In preparation for the first president's birthday celebration, the bell's crack was drilled out and widened. This was supposed to keep the edges from vibrating against each other and causing further damage. According to a newspaper account, on February 23, 1846, the bell rang out loud and clear—at first. Then, at noon, "it received a sort of compound fracture in a zigzag direction through one of its sides." The new crack "put it completely out of tune and left it a mere wreck of what it was." The old bell had rung for the last time.

From that time on, the bell became a patriotic symbol. By then, the State House had become widely known as Independence Hall, and the bell was frequently called the Liberty Bell. That name grew popular after an antislavery booklet, entitled "The Liberty Bell," used a drawing of the bell to symbolize freedom from slavery.

Visitors of all ages love touching the Liberty Bell's jagged crack.

In 1876, Philadelphia held a grand Centennial Exposition to celebrate one hundred years of independence. In preparation, city leaders removed the bell from its tower and put it on display in Independence Hall. The Liberty Bell was a huge success with the thousands of visitors who came to the exposition.

The centennial celebration at Independence Hall in 1876

After that, every city that held an exposition wanted to exhibit the Liberty Bell. Over the years, the bell traveled by train to expositions in New Orleans, Chicago, Atlanta, Charleston, Boston, St. Louis, and San Francisco. Crowds lined the railroad tracks along the bell's routes, eager to catch a glimpse of it. Each city welcomed the bell with parades, speeches, and ceremonies. Everywhere it went, the Liberty Bell was admired as a symbol of freedom.

The Liberty Bell toured the country aboard a special railroad car.

Some Philadelphians became concerned about the effect of so much travel on the bell. They worried that all the moving might damage the Liberty Bell and lengthen its crack. As a result, city officials refused San Francisco's request for the bell in 1915. However, when 200,000 California schoolchildren signed a petition asking for the bell, the officials changed their minds.

Special precautions were taken to insure the Liberty Bell's safety during the trip. Engineers designed and installed a six-armed device called a spider. The iron spider fit inside the bell and evenly supported its weight with six curved arms clamped to the bell's lip. The Liberty Bell's trip to San Francisco was its last journey outside Philadelphia.

The Liberty Bell was the featured attraction in this San Francisco parade.

However, there were other ways for the bell's message of freedom to travel across the country. Even though the Liberty Bell could no longer ring, it was not completely silent. On February 11, 1915, the bell chimed softly when it was tapped with a special wooden mallet. The sound traveled over telephone wires from Philadelphia to San Francisco in the first coast-to-coast telephone call.

In 1927, Mrs. W. Freeland Kendrick, wife of Philadelphia's mayor, tapped the Liberty Bell to celebrate the New Year (left). On June 8, 1944, a ceremony was held to mark D-Day (below).

Next, to celebrate 150 years of independence, the bell was tapped with a rubber-tipped golden mallet at the stroke of the New Year, 1926. At that moment, radio broadcasts carried the bell's voice across the country for the first time. Then, on D-Day, June 6, 1944, American armed forces began the invasion to liberate Europe from the Nazis. At dawn on that day, Philadelphia's mayor tapped the Liberty Bell with a wooden mallet. Its voice called out over the radio once again, proclaiming precious liberty.

In 1950, the city of Philadelphia agreed to let the National Park Service take charge of the Liberty Bell and Independence Hall. The Park Service created Independence National Historical Park, a twenty-two-acre (8.9-hectare) area surrounding Independence Hall. Independence Hall and other historic buildings in the area were restored. Buildings without historical importance were torn down. A modern visitor center was built. The entire area was landscaped and turned into a beautiful park.

The Liberty Bell remained at Independence Hall until 1976. That year marked the two hundredth birthday of the United States. Philadelphia expected millions of visitors during

Throughout the 1950s and 1960s, the Liberty Bell and Independence Hall were popular attractions among Philadelphia tourists.

In 1976, the Liberty Bell moved to a new home. It sits across a park from Independence Hall.

the bicentennial year. Officials decided to relocate the bell to its own glass-enclosed pavilion across the street from Independence Hall. The new home would make it easier for large crowds of people to visit it.

However, the Park Service first had to make certain that the move wouldn't damage the Liberty Bell. In a process that lasted seven and a half hours, technicians took X-ray photos of the bell. The photographs showed previously unknown minor cracks near the top of the bell and in the clapper. After evaluating all the information, engineers decided that it was safe to move the bell. At 12:01 A.M. on January 1, 1976, the Liberty Bell was transferred to its new glass pavilion.

An X-ray photo of the Liberty Bell

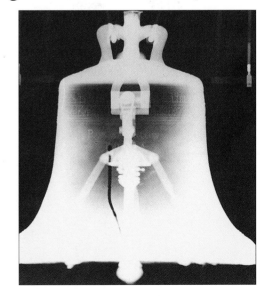

On July 4, 1976, Philadelphia celebrated the two hundredth birthday of the United States with spectacular parades and fireworks. President Gerald Ford gave a speech at Independence Hall. Two days later, on July 6, Queen Elizabeth II of England dedicated the Bicentennial Bell, a gift from her country to the United States. The Bicentennial Bell is inscribed with the words, "Let Freedom Ring!" It hangs in a 130-foot-high (40 meters) tower near the visitor center and rings twice a day.

Ringing the Liberty Bell had been a popular way of celebrating the Fourth of July until around 1860. Then, it fell out of favor, due to the increased use of fireworks. A century later, a movement began to bring back bell ringing on July Fourth.

A ceremony held in front of Independence Hall on July 4, 1976, celebrating the country's bicentennial

In February 1963, Congress passed a resolution that "bells should be rung on the holiday and that civic and other community leaders should take appropriate steps to encourage public participation in such observance."

President John F. Kennedy

A few months later, President John F. Kennedy issued a proclamation supporting bell ringing on the Fourth of July. He said, "Bells mark significant events in men's lives. Birth and death, war and peace are tolled. Bells summon the community to take note of things which affect the life and destiny of its people. The Liberty Bell rang to tell the world of the birth of a new country's freedom. Next Thursday, the Fourth of July, when the bells ring again, think back on those who lived and died to make our country free. And then resolve with courage and determination to keep it free and make it greater."

Nowadays on July Fourth, descendants of the signers of the Declaration of Independence gather at the Liberty Bell. At 2:00 P.M. Eastern time, they tap the bell to signal the start of four minutes of nationwide bell ringing.

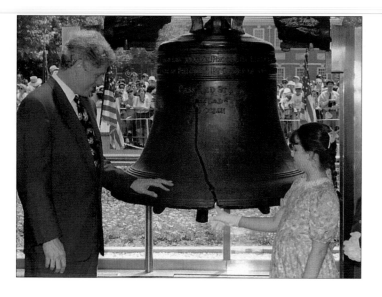

Replicas of the Liberty Bell are sometimes used to celebrate important patriotic events. President George Bush presented a replica of the Liberty Bell to Czechoslovakia in 1990 to mark that country's first anniversary of freedom from communist rule. President Bill Clinton rang a replica of the bell for his presidential inauguration in January 1993.

Early in 1995, Philadelphia's leaders suggested improvements to the area around Independence Hall and the Liberty Bell. The proposal calls for the building of a high-tech, underground museum. The museum would feature two theaters, electronic exhibits, and computer games about the Constitution and the Declaration of Independence. If the National Park Service approves the plan, the Liberty Bell will move to a new glass-and-steel pavilion about a block from its present location.

One and a half million people visit the Liberty Bell each year. Young and old, male and female, from every corner of the globe, they come to see the famous symbol of freedom.

Forty boys in identical red shirts join the crowd around the Liberty Bell. They are a choir from Ohio. Inspired by the sight of the bell, the boys begin to sing "America." The other visitors hush and listen. There are tears in many eyes as the words of the song fade away.

"My country, 'tis of thee, sweet land of liberty...
from every mountainside, let freedom ring!"

GLOSSARY

ammunition – objects fired from guns, such as bullets, musket balls, and cannon balls

Auschwitz – a Nazi concentration camp where three million people were murdered during World War II

Bicentennial celebration

bicentennial – a two hundredth birthday or anniversary

capital – a city where the government of a state or country is located

capitol – a building in which a legislature meets

cast – to shape liquid metal by pouring into a mold

centennial – a one hundredth birthday or anniversary

clapper – the tongue, or metal ball, inside a bell; when it hits the sides of the bell, the bell rings

communism – a system of government in which the state owns all property and maintains strict control over the people

D-Day – June 6, 1944—the Allied forces began the liberation of Europe during World War II

exposition – a large public display or show

inscription – the words engraved on a monument, medal, or coin

legislature – a group of people responsible for making laws for a state or country

pavilion – a light-filled, roofed building

petition – a formal, written request made to a person or group in authority

slavery – a practice in which people own other people; slavery was outlawed in the U.S. in 1865

symbol – an object that represents an idea; the Liberty Bell is a symbol of freedom

The Liberty Bell is a symbol of freedom.

TIMELINE

1751 State House Bell ordered from England
1752 State House Bell cracks during test ringing
1753 Pass and Stow recast bell twice

July 4:
Congress
approves
Declaration of
Independence

1775
1776 } American
Revolutionary War
1783
1787 U.S. Constitution written

July 8:
Bell rings at first
public reading of
Declaration of
Independence

1835

Bell cracks further **1846**
while ringing for George
Washington's birthday

Bell cracks while
tolling death of
Chief Justice
John Marshall

1885
} Liberty Bell travels
throughout
United States
1915

Bell rings as
part of first
coast-to-coast
telephone call

1926 150th birthday of U.S.; bell is heard
over radio

1939
World War II { **1944** *June 6:* D-Day; bell is heard over radio
1945

1950 National Park Service takes charge of
Liberty Bell and Independence Hall

200th birthday of U.S.; bell moves to **1976**
pavilion across from Independence Hall

Philadelphia's leaders propose moving **1995**
Liberty Bell to a new permanent pavilion

DEDICATION
For Eric

INDEX *(**Boldface** page numbers indicate illustrations.)*

PHOTO CREDITS

Cover, AP/Wide World; 1, The Historical Society of Pennsylvania; 2, Cameramann International, Ltd.; 3, UPI/Bettmann; 4, SuperStock; 7 (top), The Historical Society of Pennsylvania; 7 (bottom), AP/Wide World; 8, UPI/Bettmann; 10, Stock Montage, Inc.; 11, 12 (bottom), Bettmann Archive; 12 (top), North Wind Picture Archives; 13, The Historical Society of Pennsylvania; 15 (top), Architect of the Capitol; 15 (bottom), UPI/Bettmann; 17, North Wind; 18 (left), J. Blank/H. Armstrong Roberts; 18 (right), R. Krubner/H. Armstrong Roberts; 19, Cameramann International, Ltd.; 20, North Wind; 21, 22, 23 (bottom), The Historical Society of Pennsylvania; 23 (top), Bettmann Archive; 24, 25 (bottom), AP/Wide World; 25 (top), Lawrence S. Williams/H. Armstrong Roberts; 26, UPI/Bettmann; 27, AP/Wide World; 28 (left), Bettmann; 28 (right), UPI/Bettmann; 29, J. Nettis/H. Armstrong Roberts; 30 (top), UPI/Bettmann; 30 (bottom), SuperStock; 31 (both pictures), North Wind

STAFF

Project Editor: Sarah DeCapua
Design & Electronic Composition: TJS Design
Photo Editor: Jan Izzo
Cornerstones of Freedom Logo: David Cunningham

ABOUT THE AUTHOR

Gail Sakurai always wanted to be a writer, ever since she learned to read as a child. She planned to have her first book published by the time she was thirteen! However, for many years, other interests and needs interfered with her writing. Ms. Sakurai's childhood dream finally came true when her first book was published in 1994—only twenty-nine years later than originally planned! The book was *Peach Boy*, a retelling of a traditional Japanese legend.

Gail Sakurai lives in Cincinnati, Ohio, with her husband and two sons. When she is not writing, she enjoys spending time with her family, listening to classical music, and, of course, reading. She is a full member of the Society of Children's Book Writers and Illustrators.